Why Can't Grandma Remember My Name?

Kent L. Karosen

Chana Stiefel

Fisher Center for Alzheimer's Research Foundation
110 East 42nd St., New York, NY 10017
(800) 259-4636

Artwork created by kindergarten and first grade students at
Little Kinderartists (Rochester, New York) and Opening Minds through Art (Scripps
Gerontology Center at Miami University in Ohio), an organization that promotes
social engagement, autonomy, and dignity of people with Alzheimer's disease and
dementia by providing creative self-expression opportunities through art.

Front Cover Image: Sabrina, Age 6
Back Cover Image: George, Age 65+

Distributed by Book Baby

Acknowledgements

I would like to thank Dr. Paul Greengard, Nobel Laureate 2000 in Medicine / Physiology, and his amazing team for continuing to work to conquer Alzheimer's, as well as Dr. Barry Reisberg for his advances in patient care. I am also so grateful for the support of our friends, Brian Hauserman, Howard Lutnick, Ursula von Rydingsvard, Barry Sloane, Murray Rubin, Dick Duane, Bob Thixton, Victoria Russotti and her students at Little Kinderartists, as well as the essential contributions of Elizabeth Lokon and the artists at Opening Minds through Art program at the Scripps Gerontology Center at Miami University in Ohio. This book would not have been possible without the Fisher Foundation team in their goal of solving the mysteries of this disease. To the Board of the Foundation for their resolve and efforts, sincerest thanks to all of you.

Kent L. Karosen

Nobel Laureate
Dr. Paul Greengard,
Director of The Fisher
Center for Alzheimer's
Research

Alzheimer's disease affects far too many people across the globe. That is why I have spent much of my life conducting scientific research to understand the cause and cure for Alzheimer's disease. The disease and the debilitating effects on its victims are quite complicated and difficult to grasp. It is unique in the way it impacts and weighs on the loved ones of the patients, as well. It can be an especially difficult and confusing journey for children to witness and experience. That is why I am so proud to be the Director of the Fisher Center for Alzheimer's Research and applaud the Fisher Foundation in this endeavor to explain this disease to children in a meaningful and creative way.

Ursula von Rydingsvard

I have spent my life and career as an artist. Creating large-scale sculptures, primarily from cedar beams, has been the basis of my art career over the past 30 years. Making art not only heals me in many ways, but also brings me joy. Whether they are viewing or creating the art themselves, Alzheimer's patients can use art as a form of expression. *Why Can't Grandma Remember My Name?* is a children's book that helps to describe Alzheimer's disease for children whose loved ones are affected by the disease. The book includes pictures painted by kindergarten and first grade students, as well as art created by those afflicted with Alzheimer's. To see these works of art juxtaposed in this way provides a unique glimpse into how the mind interprets the world and provides an inspiring platform for parents to enlighten their children.

To learn more about the art created by Ursula von Rydingsvard, please visit http://www.ursulavonrydingsvard.net.

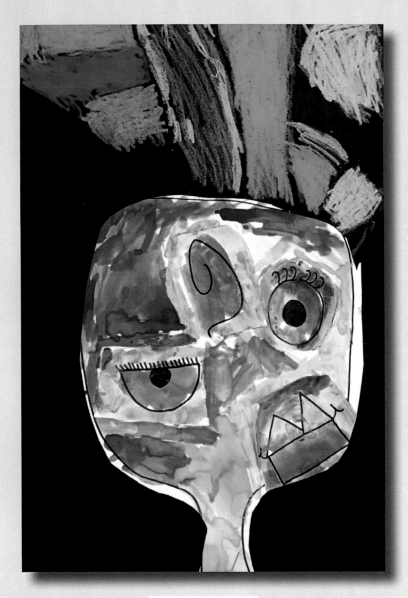

Emily, Age 4

A few weeks ago, Grandma could not find her keys. I found them in the freezer. Then she forgot about our play date in the park. I said we could go another time.

But yesterday, Grandma could not remember my name. That made me very sad. Grandma doesn't seem like "Grandma" anymore.

Is she okay?

Lenny, Age 65+

Many older people forget things from time to time. That is a normal part of aging. But sometimes memory loss can be more serious.

Grandma visited her doctor and had tests done. The doctor found out that Grandma has an illness called Alzheimer's disease.

What is Alzheimer's disease?

Alexandra, Age 9

Artist Unknown, Age 65+

Alzheimer's is a disease of the brain that makes people forget things and act differently. A German doctor named Alois Alzheimer first discovered the disease in 1906.

What causes Alzheimer's disease?

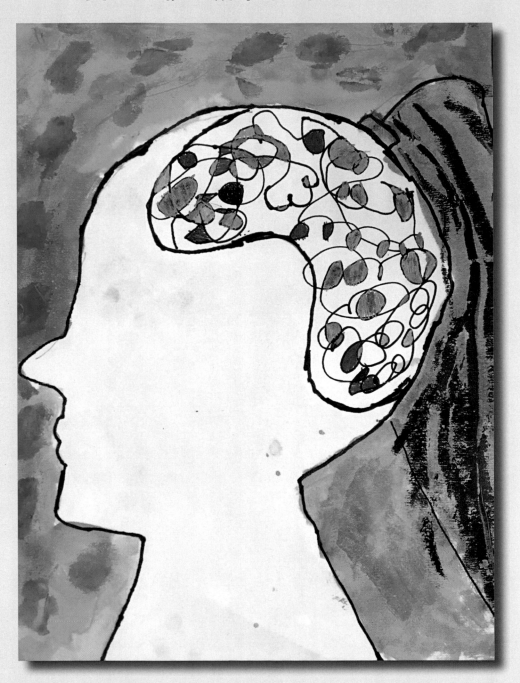

Audrey, Age 6

Bessie, Age 65+

Scientists still do not know exactly what triggers Alzheimer's, but they are studying the brain very hard to find out and to find a cure.

How does the brain normally work?

Sabrina and Audrey, Age 6

Sylvia, Age 65+

The human brain acts kind of like a computer.
It controls how our bodies work. It stores
memories and controls how we think, move, feel,
act, and sense the world around us. The brain
is made of 100 billion nerve cells, tiny building
blocks that send signals around the body.

Why isn't Grandma's brain working like usual?

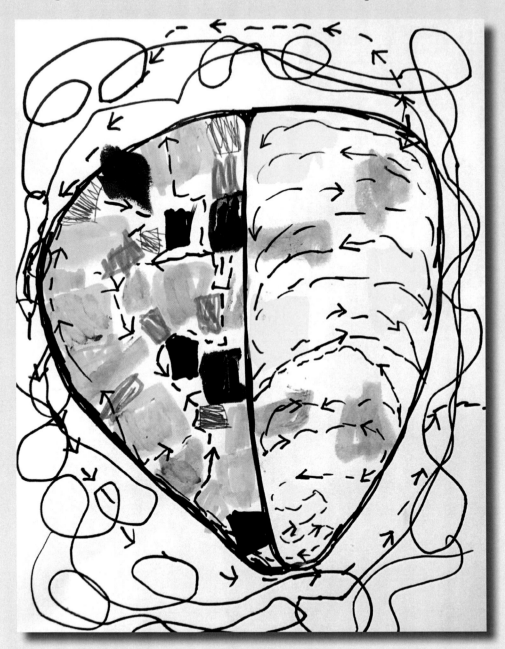

Sabrina, Age 6

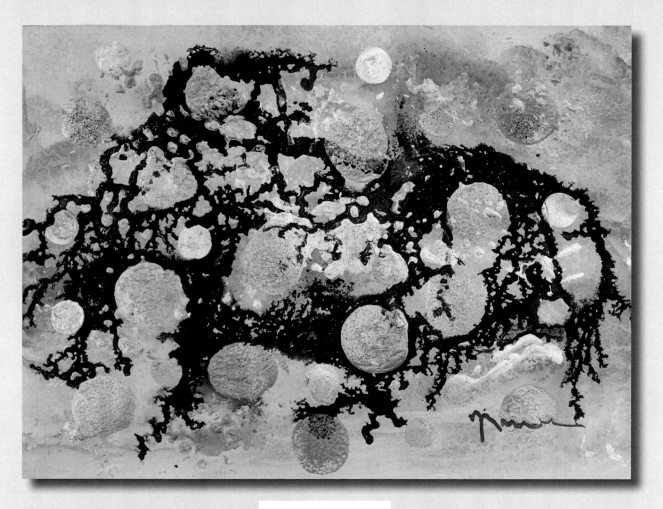

Nina, Age 65+

Scientists don't know for sure. But they have found two "prime suspects" that cause trouble in the brain of Alzheimer's patients. These substances are called plaques and tangles. They block brain cells from doing their job. That leads to memory loss and other difficulties linked to Alzheimer's.

Are there medicines to make Grandma better?

Alexandra, Age 9

Dave, Age 65+

Right now, there are some medicines that slow down the disease. Scientists hope that one day new medicines will prevent the disease.

Can I catch Alzheimer's disease from Grandma, or can you?

Will, Age 11

Artist Unknown, Age 65+

No, Alzheimer's disease is not contagious.
You can't catch it like a cold.

Do many people have this disease?

First Grade Artists

Artist Unknown, Age 65+

Yes. More than five million Americans are living with the same disease as Grandma.

Grandma sometimes gets angry.
She was never like that before. What's going on?

Noah, Age 7

Artist Unknown, Age 65+

Grandma doesn't mean to act mad. Her brain isn't working the way it used to. Alzheimer's can affect people in different ways. Some people with Alzheimer's act moody or angry. They might become very quiet and sleepy. Grandma might have trouble making plans or finishing things that she started, like preparing dinner, playing a game, or making a phone call. She might forget simple words or talk funny. Sometimes people with Alzheimer's get lost or confused. They might need help getting places. Grandma may also need help making decisions, like choosing the right clothing to wear on a hot or cold day. If you notice any of these behaviors while you're with Grandma, know that it's part of the disease. It's a good idea to talk about these signs with a grown up.

Will Grandma get worse?

Ethan, Age 6

Dave, Age 65+

Over time, Grandma will become more forgetful. She may also get more moody. She will need more help as time goes on. The best thing we can do is to be patient and be there for her when she needs us most.

How can I have fun with Grandma?

First Grade Artists

Evelyne, Age 65+

Try to do things together that Grandma still enjoys. Paint pictures, take a walk with Grandma, make collages, and enjoy a special treat with her. Play music and sing songs together.
You may enjoy making a scrapbook or album of family photos and sharing it with Grandma.

Will Grandma still be able to do things for herself?

Sabrina, Age 6

Cora, Age 65+

Life will become more challenging for Grandma.
But she can still do some things for herself.
We need to have patience with her. Many people
with Alzheimer's enjoy creating beautiful artwork.
This kind of activity makes people feel calm,
happy, and proud. Maybe you can do it with her!

Can Grandma still live at home?

Brody, Age 6

Jean, Age 65+

Some people with Alzheimer's live at home with someone who can help them. Others move to a place where they can get special care. When the time comes, we will figure out what is best for Grandma.

What else will make life better for Grandma?

Little Kinder Artist, Age 5

LaVerne, Age 65+

Show Grandma how much you love her. Give her hugs and hold her hand. She may have changed, but she will always be your Grandma.

The love that we share in our hearts will last forever.

About The Authors

Kent L. Karosen is the President and CEO of the Fisher Center for Alzheimer's Research Foundation. He also serves as a Managing Director/Partner of Cantor Fitzgerald, LP in the office of the Chairman. Born in Kansas City, he is a graduate from Kenyon College with a degree in History with an extensive study in Economics. He is also on the Board of The Intrepid Museum Foundation where he serves as the Chairman of the Investment Committee. Additionally, he is a member of the Board of Temple Emanu-El Synagogue in Miami Beach, Florida. In 2001, Kent was named an Honorary Commodore in the United States Coast Guard Auxiliary for the First Southern Region.

Chana Stiefel has written more than 20 books for children. She has a Master's degree in Science, Health, & Environmental Reporting from NYU. Chana would like to dedicate this book to her grandmother, "Bubby" Molly Epstein, who has been living with Alzheimer's for many years.
Visit Chana at: **www.chanastiefel.com.**

FISHER CENTER FOR
ALZHEIMER'S
RESEARCH FOUNDATION

About the Fisher Center for Alzheimer's Research Foundation
The Foundation was established in 1995 by Zachary Fisher to primarily fund the work of the scientists at the Fisher Center for Alzheimer's Research. The Foundation has earned and received consecutively the exceptional 4-Star rating from Charity Navigator.

The Fisher Center is one of the largest and most modern facilities in the world dedicated to solving the puzzle of Alzheimer's, and considered by many to be a prototype for Alzheimer's research. The Center is led by Nobel Laureate Dr. Paul Greengard, recipient of hundreds of awards and honors throughout his career. Dr. Greengard leads a team of over 50 world-renowned scientists. To learn more about the Fisher Center's innovative research, visit our website: **www.ALZinfo.org.**